Let's Talk About Pets

Kitty Care

David and Patricia Armentrout

ROURKE PUBLISHING

www.rourkepublishing.com

www.rourkepublishing.com

Photo credits: Cover © 6493866629; Table of Contents © Utekhina Anna; Page 4 © cloki; Page 5 © Dwight Smith; Page 6 © Daniel Rajszczak, cloki; Page 7 © Monkey Business Images; Page 8 © Norman Chan; Page 9 © NatUlrich, Scantynebula; Page 10 © Tony Campbell; Page 11 © Tony Campbell; Page 12 © Ivonne Wierink; Page 13 © Luke Schmidt, Noam Armonn; Page 14 © Leslie Morris Page 15 © Mr. TopGear; Page 16 © Nina Shannon; Page 17 © CarlssonInc ; Page 18 © Tan Kian Khoon; Page 19 © Eric Isselée, Pichugin Dmitry; Page 20 © Petr Jilek; Page 21 © pixshots; Page 22 © Nataliya Kuznetsova, Tamila Aspen, Eric Isselée, Linn Currie, Tony Campbell, Kirill Vorobyev

Editor: Jeanne Sturm

Cover and page design by Nicola Stratford, bdpublishing.com

Library of Congress Cataloging-in-Publication Data

Armentrout, David, 1962-
Kitty care / David and Patricia Armentrout.
    p. cm. -- (Let's talk about pets)
Includes bibliographical references and index.
ISBN 978-1-61590-246-0 (hard cover) (alk. paper)
ISBN 978-1-61590-486-0 (soft cover)
1. Kittens--Juvenile literature. I. Armentrout, Patricia, 1960- II. Title.
SF445.7.A75 2011
636.8'07--dc22
                          2010005366

Rourke Publishing
Printed in the United States of America, North Mankato, Minnesota
033010
033010LP

www.rourkepublishing.com - rourke@rourkepublishing.com
Post Office Box 643328 Vero Beach, Florida 32964

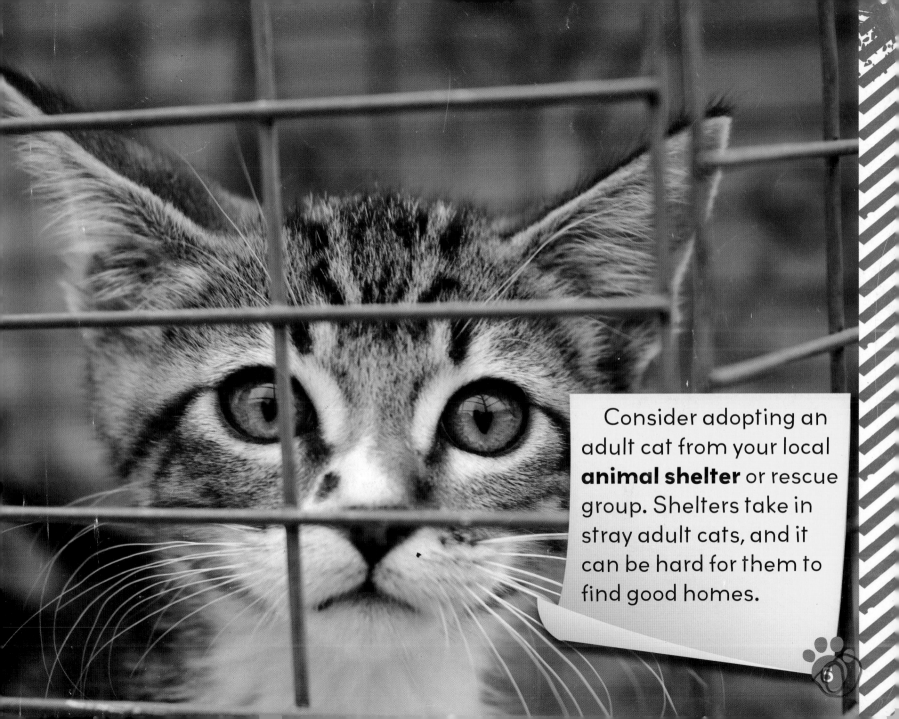

Consider adopting an adult cat from your local **animal shelter** or rescue group. Shelters take in stray adult cats, and it can be hard for them to find good homes.

A new pet means a few extra chores around the house. Don't worry. Your first job—choosing a name—can be fun. You could choose a name that matches your cat's appearance! Or, you could pick the name of a character from a favorite book or movie. Once you choose the purrfect name, use it often so your kitty gets used to hearing it.

Tiger is a good choice for a cat with orange and white stripes.

Mittens is a great name for a cat with white paws.

Your new kitty should get her first check-up from a **veterinarian** as soon as possible, within 24 to 72 hours after bringing her home.

KITTENS

There is nothing more cute and cuddly than a sleeping kitten. A kitten is, of course, a young cat. Kittens need plenty of sleep—at least 16 hours every day.

While peaceful when sleeping, kittens are little bundles of energy when they are awake. They love to romp and play. And, like other young creatures, kittens learn through play.

KITTY CORNER

Your cat has **scent glands** in his paws, and naturally scratches to mark his territory. Give him a sturdy scratching post to discourage him from using the sofa!

CAT PLAY

You can bond quickly, and earn his trust, when you play with your cat. Just remember, your cat has sharp teeth and claws. Don't play rough with your hands. Instead, give him veterinarian-approved cat toys and toss them around the room. Your cat will love *the thrill of the chase!*

Catnip is a plant from the mint family. Most cats become excited and act silly and playful when given catnip-filled toys. If your cat likes catnip, try growing some in your garden.

You may notice your cat crouches down, pounces, and swats at objects during play. The **behavior** is natural. Cats learn physical and social skills this way.

CAT CUISINE

Your kitty needs proper **nutrition** to grow up strong, happy, and healthy. You can ensure this by feeding her store-bought, prepared cat food. It can be dry, canned, or semi-moist food, as long as she gets the right amount for her weight and activity level.

Make sure your cat has fresh, clean water every day.

KITTY CORNER

Just like their big cat cousins, house cats are carnivores. That means they need to eat mostly meat.

DID YOU KNOW? . . .

Cats use their front paws as a washcloth. After each meal, they lick their paws to get them wet. Then, they rub them on places their tongues can't reach, like their ears.

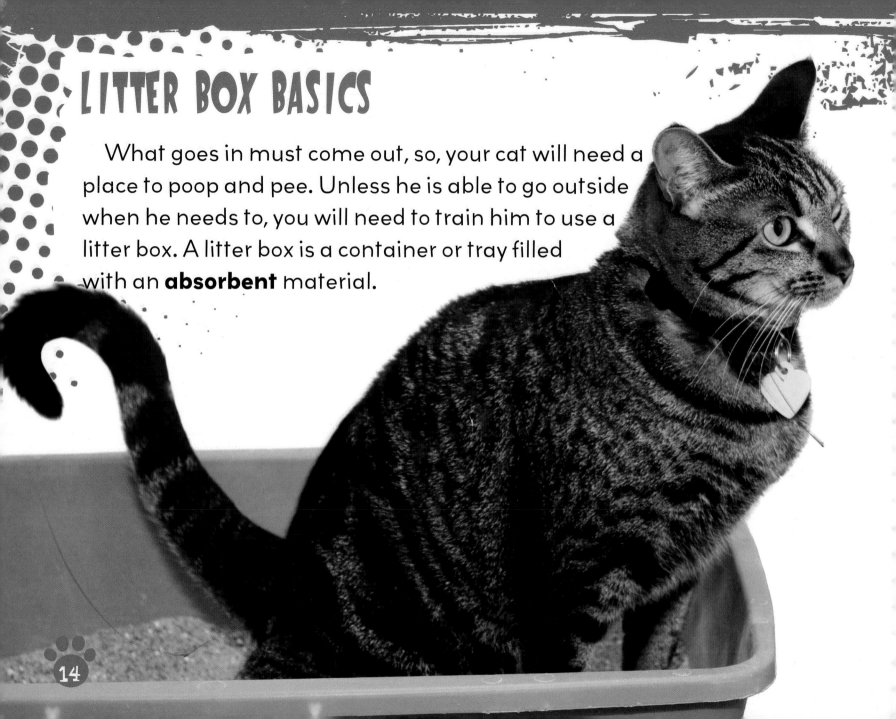

LITTER BOX BASICS

What goes in must come out, so, your cat will need a place to poop and pee. Unless he is able to go outside when he needs to, you will need to train him to use a litter box. A litter box is a container or tray filled with an **absorbent** material.

Kittens can start using a litter box when they are just a few weeks old.

Naturally hairless Sphynx kittens inspect their new litter box.

15

Place the litter box in a quiet place, away from where your cat eats and sleeps. When your cat shows signs that he needs to go, place him in the box. Praise him when he poops or pees in the box.

Poop Patrol

Cats are naturally clean animals. If their litter box is dirty, they may choose another place to go. To avoid unwanted messes, remove any clumped, dirty cat litter from the litter box as soon as you can, and replace all the litter weekly.

THE CAT'S MEOW

Cats do not talk, but they do communicate in other ways. They share feelings with sounds. Some cats meow loudly when hungry. Contented kitties **purr** softly. Scared or angry cats often **hiss**.

Cats also communicate through body language. Your cat might hold her tail high when she is happy or is saying *hello*.

She might pull her ears back against her head to warn other cats to stay away.

VET VISITS

Cats live longer and healthier lives when they see a veterinarian every year. Your veterinarian will help your family decide the kind of shots your cat needs to help him stay free from disease.

Since there are more cats than there are people who can care for them, consider it your duty to help control **overpopulation.** Your vet will explain **neutering,** a surgery for male cats, or **spaying,** a surgery for female cats.

KITTY CORNER

A tick

If your cat spends time outdoors, you should regularly check for unwanted pests like ticks and fleas.

A vet will examine your cat's eyes, ears, teeth, and gums.

KNOW YOUR CATS!

Abyssinian

American Shorthair

Maine Coon

Persian

Siamese

Sphynx

GLOSSARY

absorbent (ab-ZOR-buhnt): able to soak up liquid

animal shelter (AN-uh-muhl SHEL-tur): a temporary home for lost, stray, or unwanted animals

behavior (bi-HAYV-yuhr): doing or saying things in a certain way

hiss (HISS): to make a "ssss" noise like a snake

neutering (NOO-tur-ing): surgically removing the reproductive organs in a male animal

nutrition (noo-TRISH-uhn): food that contains all the things needed to keep animals and people healthy

overpopulation (oh-vur-pop-yuh-LAY-shuhn): too many people or animals that can be taken care of in a certain area

purr (PUR): a low, soft sound a cat makes in its throat

scent glands (SENT GLANDZ): organs that release chemicals which cats and other animals can identify

spaying (SPAY-ing): surgically removing the reproductive organs in a female animal

veterinarian (vet-ur-uh-NAIR-ee-un): a person trained to treat injured or sick animals

23

Index

Websites

www.animal.discovery.com/cat-guide/

www.aspca.org

kids.cfa.org/

www.paw-rescue.org

About the Authors

David and Patricia Armentrout live near Cincinnati, Ohio, with their two sons and dog, Max. After adopting Max in 2001, it didn't take long before he won over the hearts of family, friends, and neighbors! The Armentrouts have also had other pets over the years, including cats, birds, guinea pigs, snakes, fish, turtles, frogs, and hermit crabs.